MY
ABCs
OF LIFE

August, 2010

Bob & Wilma

A little gift for you!

Lloyd Berman

MY ABCs OF LIFE

Apply Them for Greater Success in Yours

LLOYD BURNER

TATE PUBLISHING
AND ENTERPRISES, LLC

My ABCs of Life
Copyright © 2015 by Lloyd Burner. All rights reserved.

Scripture quotations marked (KJV) are taken from the *Holy Bible, King James Version*, Cambridge, 1769. Used by permission. All rights reserved.

This book is designed to provide accurate and authoritative information with regard to the subject matter covered. This information is given with the understanding that neither the author nor Tate Publishing, LLC is engaged in rendering legal, professional advice. Since the details of your situation are fact dependent, you should additionally seek the services of a competent professional.

The opinions expressed by the author are not necessarily those of Tate Publishing, LLC.

Published by Tate Publishing & Enterprises, LLC
127 E. Trade Center Terrace | Mustang, Oklahoma 73064 USA
1.888.361.9473 | www.tatepublishing.com

Tate Publishing is committed to excellence in the publishing industry. The company reflects the philosophy established by the founders, based on Psalm 68:11,
"The Lord gave the word and great was the company of those who published it."

Book design copyright © 2015 by Tate Publishing, LLC. All rights reserved.
Cover design by Norlan Balazo
Interior design by Jomar Ouano

Published in the United States of America

ISBN: 978-1-62746-988-3
Biography & Autobiography / Religious
15.06.24

Dedicated to my grandsons, with my love.
(I had you in my thoughts as I wrote this little book.
For success in your life, apply my ABCs of life to yours).

~ MY FIVE GRANDSONS ~

Stephen (Greaves)

Andrew "Andy" (Greaves)

David (Burner)

Scott (Burner)

Nicholas "Nick" (Dineen)

Acknowledgments

To all those acquaintances and loved ones who provided an excellent example of life as it should be, teaching by example, as well as words, I will always be wholeheartedly thankful. Foremost of those being my loving and caring parents, Clyde Sr. and Veva Burner, and my siblings, Clyde Jr., Mary, Edward, John, Joe, and Ben, who would not let me be spoiled or demand my own way while growing up. My dear wife, Gale, who is more than a helpmeet to me, encouraging and considerate, patient, and the love of my life.

I want to give a special expression of love to my children, Sandra, Allen, and Gloria, as they allowed me to practice in life what I am sharing with you. My grandchildren, Stephen (who left us far too early), Andy, David, Scott, and Nick, who have let me break all the rules of parenting and love them unconditionally.

All of these have made my book possible, but I would be remiss if I failed to give a special thank you to my longtime pastor, Dr. Mel Efaw, and his family and special friends in the faith, my fellow church workers, friends and coworkers, who have added much encouragement and help.

My hardworking great-nephew Brian deserves a huge thank you, as he continues to assist us in many ways. Brian encouraged me to put my writings out where others could read them, and he also built my blog.

A thank you to others along the way who have encouraged me to continue my writing and to publish my book. And a great, big thank you to the folks at Tate Publishing company that I have had the privilege to work with and who so brilliantly produced my book.

Contents

Foreword

My dear friend of over sixty years has written this book out of a wealth of personal experience and an intimate walk with God. King Solomon, the wisest man that ever lived, wrote the books of Proverbs and Ecclesiastes in the Bible. These two books are called wisdom books because they communicate God's direction for living to man. Lloyd has also written a book of wisdom, and his source is two-fold. First, it is the Bible itself, and second, it is the application of those eternal principles found in his study of the Bible. The core values expressed in *My ABCs of Life* reflect the core values that Lloyd has gleaned from personal experience in seeking to live out God's Word.

This book is not a sermon but a warm, caring treatise from the author's heart because he cares about people and especially the young people of our country. Cultures change and along with it the people of that culture. However, God's absolutes and wisdom bridge time and change. Today's generation would do well to take heed to Lloyd's sage advice because its foundation is the unchangeable revelation from God.

I was one of the "kids" Lloyd referenced in his book whom Lloyd and his wife mentored and loved. With the writing of this book, he can keep mentoring and guiding the young people of this generation long after he has gone to His heavenly home.

Jim Efaw, Denver, Colorado

A Special Note:

Please take to heart what I am sharing with you, hide it in your heart, and put into practice all the good stuff you like and read as best you can.

Don't Let Anything Distract You!

Don't get off the track from reaching your dreams, always knowing that the Lord gives you whatever abilities and success you might achieve. In fact, we don't have anything we haven't received from him. He is the designer of your life, and provides all the needed materials for your success, but you are the primary worker. You have all the resources required for a happy life, so go for it!

You can and should put your complete trust in him.

My prayer is that you will find happiness and joy in your life.

Introduction

Your life will take some crazy, and unexpected, turns while traveling down the path the Lord has given you. I know mine has, and I have learned much from each one, wishing now that I had learned more.

I will always be thankful for the mentors I had in my life; my parents being the most important. I remember clearly the first time I met Mr. Gordon Chain, the man who was the commander of the civil air patrol cadet program in my hometown. I was in high school, and WWII was heating up. My two older brothers had already left for the military, and my only sister had gone to Washington, DC, to work. I felt sorry for my parents, sending their children off one by one. I wanted to be next, and I was excited to go. I fell in love with flying, and wanted to learn all I could about aviation.

As his car pulled up in front of my house, I was on the front porch waiting on him, and didn't waste any time getting into his car. He was taking me to my first meeting to help me join the program. He picked me up every week for over a year, helped me learn with tutoring, and set a very good example for me.

I have included something under P you will enjoy reading, "Protecting Your Inheritance." This gentleman I told you about, and several others who mentored me, surely knew how to protect theirs. Jesus said that if we wanted to find our life, we should give it away; if we keep it to ourselves, we will lose it. It's important that you find out what that means. My mentors found out, and I am confident they have been rewarded.

I have written these little thoughts primarily for younger folks, but equally apply to anyone. Since this writing is about life, and how you live it, reading my thoughts should help you from what I have learned through the years. These are simplistic in nature, but very important thoughts that I feel are basic to your success and happiness. I am still learning the game of life and will be ninety years old my next birthday. Now, that really sounds old!

If you have a good relationship with your heavenly Father, it will help you tremendously with these ABC's I have given you. I won't be preaching to you, but will be teaching you. I know from experience and from the testimony of many others though that our relationship to God is very important. I hope you agree.

Always remember that whatever endeavor you undertake can be fun and enjoyable. Endeavors connected with education, or special projects are not a matter of life or death, and you should try to enjoy doing them as much as possible.

Remember also that all of life is a game, although a much more serious game than videos or sports, but life can and should be fun too! It's important for you to know as much as you can about yourself; where you came from, and why you are here. We all came from God, so we should live to please Him. The best life manual for me is the Bible, but much of my life was learned by trial and error.

One of the most important truths to learn is that God loves you! You can find that in the Bible in the New Testament, John's Gospel message, chapter 3.

You are here because God wanted you here, and He loves you. That's good news, isn't it?

Ecclesiastes 12:13, 14: "Let us hear the conclusion of the whole matter: Fear God, and keep His commandants: for this is the whole duty of man. For God shall bring every good work into judgment, with every secret thing, whether it be good or whether it be evil."

As you learn these ABC's of Life, for complete fulfillment, remember "the full conclusion of all that matters." In other words, learn how to not sweat the small stuff, and let all that really matters be your purpose for doing all that you do. You can and will be successful. Rest assured that the Lord loves you and will take care of you in all of your endeavors!

Let me share with you some thoughts from the following question that was asked of me out of a book my oldest daughter gave me:

Question: Recall for me five of the most important lessons you have learned in life.

My Answer:

1. All that I am, have, and ever will be, comes from God; Creator, Protector, and Savior.

2. Love is the essential thing of life. To love and to be loved.

3. The greatest thing that God brought into being is the family. To be part of a family, with all of its struggles, pain, hurt, and love, is what life is all about.

4. To live by faith and not by sight. We can't control much of anything, sometimes not even ourselves. I am so very thankful for the faith He has given me.

5. That life is just the beginning, not the end, of a wonderful eternal existence, if you know Christ as your personal Savior.

To me, the most important purpose in life is to be useful, honest, and compassionate toward others. One of my favorite sayings is, "One of the smallest things on earth might be a person consumed with self." We all should try to make a

difference in our own little world and to know that you have
done the best you could. I hope you enjoy the following poem
I wrote for my family:

A Family

A family is more than a photograph,
More than a picture on the wall;
A family is love, and laughter
And hugs, with memories to recall.

A family is babies cuddly and warm,
Held securely in mother's care;
A family is fussing, and helping
And such, with lots of love to share.

A family is more than a photograph,
More than a picture on the wall;
A family is love, when sickness
Strikes, or when death makes a call.

A family is children playing,
With cousin, aunt and uncle, friend;
A family is celebrating holidays,
Hoping this good day would not end.

A family is more than a photograph,
More than a picture on the wall.

Now, start learning your ABC's.

Attitude

Commit thy works unto the LORD,
and all thy thoughts shall be established.

—Proverbs 16:3

Attitude is the place to start in your pursuit of your endeavors of life! If your attitude is out of adjustment, everything else will be also. What kind of attitude should I have, you ask?

Let your attitude be: "I Can Do This!"
I will be willing to *learn*—to be *taught*!
If it's important enough to learn and do, you must have a *positive* attitude about it!

Let Your Attitude Be: "I Can Do This!"

You will do it better, and it will be longer lasting if you "commit all you do to the Lord". But you can do it if you are mentally able, physically able, and if you want to do it badly enough.

You don't have to be the smartest person in town to have a successful life. It really depends on what you want in life; not many will be famous, and consider that a lot of the rich and famous are not the happiest folks around. Most of the happy people I have known are the ones that are content with whatever circumstance they are in. Accept the fact that intellect doesn't give you all the answers. Success is mostly obtained by good old hard work of applying yourself to the task, and sticking with it through the hard parts. It takes a good attitude.

Neither do you have to be the most physically fit person in your class, at your workplace, or even in your home. But you must have the right attitude! Always let your attitude be one of "I can do this!" We have a lot of people in the news today who have lost arms and legs in accidents, and serving in the military to protect our freedom, and they are overcoming these obstacles in remarkable ways. If you happen to have a physical problem that needs to be overcome, get your attitude in proper alignment, and you will be amazed at what you accomplish. You have to want to do it badly enough.

Whatever you do, don't let an attitude of anger overcome you. Anger is a destroyer, and it destroys the one who is angry, not the other person. You can choose to be angry when offended, or not to be. It is far better to control your anger and let your performance defeat the antagonist. Resist getting the condition I call "hardening of the attitudes."

I have seen anger destroy too many otherwise fine people. They just couldn't get past it, and it consumed them; sometimes for years, and long past remembering why they were angry in the first place.

I Will Be Willing to Learn—To Be Taught!

It is hard to like people who have the answer to everything, and willingly offer it. The only problem is that they usually have the wrong answer, and speak before they are spoken to. The tongue is your friend if used properly; if not, it can be your enemy and get you into hot water.

Some bright person has said: "Where there is no learning, there is no teaching." I think that is true, but I'll let you decide. I do know that if you really want to learn, you must be ready to be taught! Without a proper *attitude* the teacher doesn't have much of a chance, and you won't learn much. You must be willing to learn—to be taught! Kind of makes sense, doesn't it?

Maybe you know someone, and I hope it isn't you, that pretty much thinks they already know all they need to know about the subject and are hard to teach. I recall knowing a young man who was like this to some extent. It started early; his hand had to be the first one raised with the answer whether he knew it or not, and he always seemed to be in a hurry to answer before really being taught. What amazed me was that he made good grades and became a success as the world measures success, but it took him a lot longer than it should have.

Being willing to learn – to be taught is much better and will help you accomplish much more in a shorter period of time.

If It's Important Enough to Learn and Do, You Must Have a Positive Attitude About It!

"What's the big deal about having a positive attitude?" you might be thinking. Let's think about that for a minute, and see if we can come to an agreement on this. I think a positive attitude will give you a much better chance to learn how to do something properly and enjoy it, and anything else that you will need to be successful in life. Each day try to approach your tasks positively, whether you really understand all you are doing or not, and you will find that it will rub off on others, and they will be more willing to help you. I will add this: "Have a positive attitude with enthusiasm."

So let's go on, with our new attitude, this should be fun. Remember, if it's important enough to learn and do, you must have a positive attitude about it!

Yes, it all really does start with *the right attitude.*

Commit thy works unto the LORD, *and all thy thoughts shall be established.*

—Proverbs 16:3

Be You—Yourself

Wisdom is the principal thing, therefore get wisdom:
and with all thy getting get understanding.

—Proverbs 4:7

Let me explain to you what I mean by be you—yourself, and what you need to learn. Remember, you are unique, there is just one exactly like you, and there is no one else just like you. You have to figure out who you are and accept you—yourself for what you are, while deciding what you want to do in life. It's wonderful that the brain (not necessarily in size, but in intellect) grows along with the body. You must get your own wisdom, and while you are getting that, get understanding. See if there are changes that need to be made in you—yourself, and determine if you are willing to make the sacrifices necessary to get done whatever it is you want to do.

Do you recall what I said in Attitude," about learning, that you must be willing to be taught? Well:

You must be you—yourself in your pursuit of learning!
Being yourself won't make you less of a person than someone else.

You Must Be You—Yourself In Your Pursuit of Learning!

All of us learn at a different pace; some faster than others, but not necessarily better. Learning and remembering, by applying what you have learned, is best. It doesn't do much good to learn and then forget. An old adage, "If you don't use it, you lose it" is so true!

That's why it's so important to be yourself in your learning, so in getting your understanding, you won't learn like others. You are you! That's the way God has made you, and if you stop and think about it, that makes your life so much more exciting. You can be thankful that you aren't a robot, or mechanically controlled. I am so glad for that, aren't you? In fact, I want to be myself, and I want you to be you—yourself also.

If you spend too much time in front of a mirror, you will start finding defects (in your mind, you will think of them as defects) in your eyes, your hair, whatever, wishing you looked like someone else. That is a no-no, you will be much happier just being *you*!

"Be the best you can be in all that you do" is an old cliché, but it is a good one. But you might be saying, "My best just doesn't seem to be good enough." Ask yourself what it needs to be good enough for; is it good enough for you to be satisfied, to be able to go to school or work every day, and in the future provide for you and your family? Your pursuit of learning won't necessarily mean that you will be the best, or the one in the limelight. If you stop and think about it, that might be best for you. Most folks wouldn't be happy if they were constantly in the limelight, although you might think you would.

Being Yourself Won't Make You Less of a Person Than Someone Else

I knew a young man once who really made a great effort to emulate and be just like his idol. He failed to do that because it was impossible. He was frustrated and confused as to why he wasn't succeeding, until he realized what he was doing. He was really making himself less of a person; when he started being himself, he was more of a person! He started using his own wisdom and his own understanding.

Through the years, I've known folks who tried to conduct themselves in business and in school like others they looked up to. It didn't work for them and it won't work for you. Be more of a person, be you—yourself.

It is wise to learn from others, if you watch them to learn from their mistakes, and what they do to succeed, but your actions and methods will be yours, it won't be theirs. One of the things that helped me was that I learned to watch those who I respected and admired; seeing how they performed; studying and applying that knowledge and treating those around them with dignity and respect. What they did was theirs, and mine wasn't always as good as theirs, but it helped me to learn from them, and not try to become them.

> *Wisdom is the principal thing, therefore get wisdom:*
> *and with all thy getting get understanding.*

—Proverbs 4:7

Capture the Moment

My son, attend to my words;
incline thine ear unto my sayings.

—Proverbs 4:20

Don't hesitate to listen to good instruction
Remember, he who hesitates, can be left behind
The moments are fleeting

Don't Hesitate to Listen to Good Instruction

I will remind you of this again, because I don't want you to fall into the trap of *not listening*. Its human nature I guess to think we already have all the answers, but whatever you do, don't hesitate to listen to good instruction.

I say "good" because not all of the instruction you get will be good. Some of it is downright bad; you have to be careful who you listen to and who you do not listen to. It is great that you have the ability to *tune them out*, but be very careful not to tune the good ones out too quickly!

Young people have a way of tuning out their parents, and that's too bad. Parents have the benefit of experience, of trying out life, and it's usually best to listen attentively to their words. They aren't perfect, and the advice they give isn't always the best, or it might not be what you wanted to hear, but you will benefit by listening to them and learning.

In capturing your moment, a decision you make in that moment can change your entire life. For instance, while reading this you might suddenly realize that you need to consider seriously some of these thoughts I am passing on to you, and you decide to do something about it. That decision could change you for the rest of your life, and for the better I hope.

A decision to go with the wrong crowd, or to the wrong place, and knowing it is wrong, could change your entire direction in life. Think before you decide.

Remember, He Who Hesitates Can Be Left Behind

First, I tell you not to hesitate, and now I tell you if you hesitate, you will lose. What is going on here? Well, there is a time to hesitate and a time that you shouldn't. What I'm trying to remind you of here is when an opportunity to grow and is something you want to pursue presents itself, please don't wait too long or it will be gone. This is especially true in pursuing your life endeavors, and it can come up in your home life and schoolwork.

You will be making many important decisions for the direction of your life; some can and should be, be made with a lot of prayer and thought, while others need immediate action. It's serious business when you fall into the trap of hesitating and not going ahead with what you know you need to do. You can make *decent* grades, but could do much better if you don't put off studying. Don't put things off until the last minute; you know what happens when you do that—less than your best, so don't let that happen.

Putting off until the last minute will definitely hurt you; you have given over control to chance or whatever was left over when you could have been in complete control. Hesitating can leave you behind. Plan ahead, make wise choices, and act on what you need to do.

The Moments are Fleeting

Capture the moment, because it's amazing how fast time flies. We all have the same amount of time, and when you are young, it doesn't concern you too much. As you age, you will find yourself wondering where all of it went. Use each moment wisely, those minutes makeup the hours that fill up the days! Listen, learn, apply your knowledge, and follow through on finishing the task at hand. Capture the Moment!

My son, attend to my words;
incline thine ear unto my sayings.

—Proverbs 4:20

Determination with Discipline

Now therefore give me this mountain.

—Joshua 14:12a

Determine in your heart to succeed
We all need discipline in our lives
We might need to discipline others

Determine In Your Heart to Succeed

Caleb, in the Old Testament book of Joshua, was eighty-five years old and was still able to determine in his heart to take another mountain. Regardless of your age or circumstances, you can have this same kind of determination. Just "keep on, keeping on" and you will be amazed what you can accomplish.

The satisfaction of accomplishment is worth the doing! You might not think so now if it is not going too well for you, but believe me, it is. All of the most successful people have said that the activity of doing the job that brought them to the top was far more satisfying than being at the top. They all started looking at the next project to conquer.

What keeps great people on top? Do you think it is the "being on top" that does it? That's part of it, I'm sure, but he/she has to work hard every day to continue to improve. Improve? Yes, the successful ones know that whatever they are doing is never completely learned and it can leave them quickly if they don't stay on top of it. They are willing to continue their education, and doing above and beyond what is expected of them. They enjoy the doing and it works. I read recently of a ninety-five-year-old man who was an accomplished cellist, and recognized as one of the world's finest. When asked why he practiced several hours a day, at his age, he responded, (not verbatim), "Well, I think I'm still progressing." In fact, we never stop learning as long as we can think, and want to.

Now think of what you are striving at for a moment, and it isn't going too well for you. It could be that you are trying too hard. What do you do? First of all, you want to continue, and enjoy it as much as you can, just don't give up. Follow a few steps given you here:

Get back to the basics; analyze mentally where you are and what you are doing.

Zero in on what is giving you the most trouble.

Get to resources that can help you the most, and don't hesitate to talk to others who can help you.

Concentrate on that one area and work it out.

Whatever it costs you will be well worth it. Once you get it straightened out, keep doing it until it becomes a part of you again as it once was.

It might be that your problem is in your work, later on, your marriage, your relationships, your children (when you have them), whatever? Apply the same logic as above—get back to the basics; analyze mentally your situation; and zero in on what is giving you the most trouble. Open up to others being affected by your actions, and you can possibly solve the problem right then and there.

We All Need Discipline In Our Lives

Children need proper training, and discipline is an important factor in our development. Try to imagine a world where everyone is doing their own thing, whenever and however they want to.

Discipline is needed in our schools, our homes, our military, and our work place; without it we could not get much done. We see a lack of discipline today in our cities where there is violence against authority. It is a very unpleasant place to be, and people are hurt or killed.

Believe me, discipline is a very good thing.

We Might Need To Discipline Others

There came a time when I had to discipline my children. In the future, this could be true for you too. Have you been around a kid that wasn't disciplined properly? Have you seen the temper tantrums, the kicking, and screaming until they got what they wanted? It wasn't a very pleasant sight was it? I had to discipline, so the example my parents gave me helped me understand how important it was in my children's lives.

Discipline produces order in our lives, control over our emotions and actions that sometimes come into play, and could get us into trouble without discipline.

Don't hesitate to accept discipline and to apply it when appropriate.

Now therefore give me this mountain.

—Joshua 14:12a

Energize the Moment

But God hath chosen the foolish things of the world to confound the wise; and God hath chosen the weak things of the world to confound the things which are mighty.

—1 Corinthians 1:27

Don't be surprised when you energize!
Bring energy to every endeavor
Don't waste your energy

Don't Be Surprised When You Energize!

With your new attitude, being you yourself, and chasing your dream, you will energize the moment! It can't help happening, and it will be exciting. You will find that after learning the basics and sticking with them, you can work miracles in whatever you do.

You might be shocked, but you shouldn't be too surprised, because energizing should become a part of you. Try to make it a part of you, as natural as breathing. That sounds good, doesn't it, but how do you do it?

Put energy into your learning, your practice, and your life. In every endeavor, and in all of life, it takes energy, lots of it. Most aren't able or willing to come up with enough to excel. Most are satisfied to *just get by*. To me, and I hope to you, that just isn't enough. But it is a matter of priorities; remember to put the important things in your life first—not all are that high on the list right now; your love of God, and your education and career are—make those your number one priority.

On your next project, try to do a little bit better than you have, or it might be that you need to do a whole lot better if you have gotten lazy. Prove to yourself what a little extra energy will do; improve your attitude, realize that God has made you uniquely, and you can chase your dream. Just don't be surprised when you energize!

Bring Energy To Every Endeavor

Have you seen someone who has a lot of talent to accomplish things, but do less than their best? Someone who seems to go at things hesitatingly, or without the energy needed to succeed? Their success rate could be much higher if they brought more energy into the endeavor.

The following example is mentioned to illustrate how one of my growing up friends used his God-given energy to help him win, while limiting his endurance by hurting his body.

When I was just a teen, probably about fifteen, Jackie moved into our neighborhood, and I knew right away that he was different from the rest of us. Jackie was full of energy. This is something *that I shouldn't have been impressed with, and I hope your aren't either,* but he impressed all us younger guys, because he could chew tobacco and smoke a cigarette at the same time (this is wasted energy and a destroyer of health, but seemed to be the thing to do back then). He was a couple years older than me, and being young and foolish, I had started playing around with cigarettes. I looked up to Jackie (a big mistake). He wasn't very big, but he was pretty cool, and he brought a lot of energy into every endeavor (too bad it wasn't the good kind of energy). This made up for his lack of size when it came to competing with the older and bigger boys, and he could outrun most of the other boys. I don't know what happened to Jackie, he was good at playing games and all the other stuff he did, but that didn't get him very far in life. He wasn't doing much of anything the last I knew of him.

But back to the real world. What are you going to do with the God-given energy you have? You know it takes a lot of energy to do the job at school or at work, but what about those things you pursue in life? Your energy needs to be used in learning, and then in practicing what you have learned.

Concentration and staying focused takes considerable energy, and these are two of the most important parts of your life.

I'm thankful I quit smoking when I was twenty-seven years old when I asked Christ into my life. He took tobacco, drinking, and cursing out of my life for which I have been thankful every day. My energy was being sapped by my lifestyle, and He restored it for me. I couldn't do it by myself. I hope tobacco didn't finish Jack off at an early age, but it has many that I have known, so stay away from it.

Smoking cigarettes or chewing tobacco won't make you any more of a man, but it might kill you. Like all sin, we feel guilt while doing it, and it doesn't glorify the Lord, and it takes as much or more of our energy as good productive stuff.

I want you to bring good, God-given energy into your every endeavor.

Don't Waste Your Energy

We had horse-drawn wagons delivering milk and ice on our street when I was a boy growing up. I never saw one of those horses waste his energy. He knew the route better than his driver, I think, and went just as far as he had to, to make the delivery. He stood still while the driver was away, and moved at his own pace after starting up again. Come to think of it, the driver was using his energy wisely also as he had spent lots of time training his horse, which was helping him do a better job.

You would be wise to learn from the horse and driver. There will be times you will need an extra burst of energy, but when it is over, conserve your energy by being well prepared and with proper rest. Use your energy wisely by breathing properly, maintaining a good working weight, eating slowly, and drinking lots of water; just don't let bad habits creep in that 'cause you to waste your energy.

Let me tell you about my older brother Edward, and one way not to use your energy. Ed found out that he liked to fight. He was tough and liked to mix it up with anyone that got in his way. He had the energy all right, but it was being wasted. He had whipped about everyone he had fought, so he decided he could whip our dad, which was a big mistake. Ed found out that even his tough look and energy couldn't overcome experience and speed. My dad had been brought up in the mountains of West Virginia, was six-foot one, and weighed 170 pounds, but he was muscular, lean, and knew a little about fighting. Ed came in after a weekend of carousing with his friends. My mother was distraught and worried about him. He confronted dad, and when dad questioned him about where he had been, he put his fist up in a fighting stance and dared dad to fight him. Dad didn't really want to hit him, but knew he had to teach him a lesson. Before Ed could make a move, dad gave him a couple quick blows, and Ed went flying across the floor to the other side of the linoleum-covered kitchen. He was like a whipped puppy, not really knowing what had hit him. That was the last time he took on dad.

I always looked up to Ed, even though he thumped me plenty of times. He finally got his energy directed in a more productive way and was successful in his work, did a good job raising a family, and became a pretty good golfer as well.

> *But God hath chosen the foolish things of the world to confound the wise; and God hath chosen the weak things of the world to confound the things which are mighty.*
>
> —1 Corinthians 1:27

Forgetting and Moving Forward!

Forgetting

Brethren, I count not myself to have apprehended: but this one thing I do, forgetting those things which are behind, and reaching forth unto those things which are before.

—Philippians 3:13

Forget those past mistakes!
What is it you are forgetting?

Moving Forward!
Forget Those Past Mistakes

As quickly as you can I might add! Forgetting? I thought you were talking about learning and remembering! Okay, you're right, but the point I want to make is to forget those past mistakes, although I know from experience that they can't be forgotten completely. It is much easier if you turn them over to the Lord and ask Him to help you. I'm glad that His forgetter works better than ours.

You have to remember that a big percentage of anything you do becomes a mind game. If you do something well, and then lose your concentration, gloating in your new found ability, you will probably mess up terribly on the very next try. This can be devastating if you aren't mentally prepared for it.

Messing up in life can have the same bad effect or worse. You might be sailing along doing pretty good, and suddenly do something really stupid that sets you back. You are embarrassed and have to make amends. Admit your error; confess it to the Lord, asking His forgiveness, and any others that you have offended. So now what do you do? The secret is in forgetting, read on.

What Is It You Are Forgetting

You can't redo the past that is done and gone. Forget it. Just don't forget the important things. You can forget the bad stuff but whatever you do, don't forget the stuff you need to do and know.

This used to be one of my parents' favorite questions when I was about to go out the door before I was really ready to go, "What is it you are forgetting? Being wiser they knew that in my haste, I had overlooked something I needed, like my books, or my coat, or to comb my hair.

Funny thing, my teachers asked me the same question while looking at the incomplete paper I was turning in. It usually caught me off guard and was embarrassing. I needed to start focusing on the important thing, on the problem or project I had in front of me.

And moving forward!

Don't settle for neutral, as you will be going backwards—keep moving forward. Yes, you will not always be successful, there will be times when you will have to make adjustments to do better, but whatever you do, keep going on, move forward. Keep on growing, not only physically, but mentally, spiritually, in every way. It is an important part of your maturing.

Brethren, I count not myself to have apprehended: but this one thing I do, forgetting those things which are behind, and reaching forth unto those things which are before.

—Philippians 3:13

Grow In Your Inner Self

Speaking the truth in love,
may grow up into Him in all things.

—Ephesians 4:15a

No one is standing still, if you aren't growing, you are going backward. Going backward means you are losing ground, and none of us wants that.

Grow spiritually and things will fall into place for you.
Be diligent to learn and grow

Grow Spiritually and
Things Will Fall Into Place For You

After coming out of the military at the age of twenty-one, I didn't know for several years what I was going to do with my life. I floundered and wasted my precious time. I had forgotten my upbringing, as my parents had taken me and my siblings (all seven of us!) to church while growing up. I had faithfully attended Sunday school, had watched my parents change, growing spiritually and was excited when that happened.

But during my struggling time, being spiritual just wasn't too important to me, and that was too bad for me. Things sure weren't falling into place for me; in fact my life was a mess. When the Lord intervened and my life turned around, it all changed for the better. I learned that I needed to grow spiritually for things to fall into place for me, and if you want it bad enough you will also.

Suddenly everything I tried or did took on a new meaning to me. I had a desire to do my best and to succeed. Before my change, I hadn't started out in my life career yet and was still uncertain what I would do, but I had started to play sports games (as you are probably engaged in some extracurricular activity), although neither meant very much to me before I started to grow spiritually. I was just *playing around*. When my life changed for the better, all of that changed. I thought of both more seriously and enjoyed them more. I had a desire to do well; I had found purpose for my life. I hope you do as well. Note: to see the writing of my WWII experience, go to www.uncleburnie.wordpress.com.

Be Diligent to Learn and Grow

Remember, as I mentioned earlier, it's the accomplishing of the thing that is rewarding and exciting. Of course, reaching the top is great too, but it's in the getting there that you will find you like best. That's why learning and growing are so important, that's where the fun is. I know that probably right now you are saying, "Wait a minute, do you realize how hard this is?" Yes, I do, I have been there and done that. I didn't think so at the time I was learning and growing either, but looking back I know it was true.

You don't want to be left behind, and being diligent to learn and grow will keep you ahead of the pack—especially in life! You grow in your work by continuing to learn even after you have learned enough to get by, and you grow in everything you do by working on what you have learned through practice and participating. I think all levels of workers that require professional skill, have continuing education classes they must attend to keep their jobs, and to keep up with the competition.

Another way we learn and grow is when we find the benefit of working well with others.

Here is my answer to one of those questions my children asked me:

Question: Share some of your insights for working well with others.

My Answer:

Learn to laugh at yourself.

Give the other guy the benefit of the doubt.

Don't demand your own way, or that your way is the only way.

Be diligent and dependable.

Be on time and not a slouch.

Have fun and do a good job.

Be well prepared for the task and willing to help others—you have those who are helping you along the way.

Speaking the truth in love,
may grow up into Him in all things.

—Ephesians 4:15a

Head and Hands

But I would have you know,
that the head of every man is Christ.

—1 Corinthians 11:3a

Keep a steady head
Watch what your hands do, and where they go

Keep a Steady Head

If you keep a steady head in all that you do it will pay off for you. Don't let the opposition get the best of you, no matter how hard they try. Don't get mad and fight, get even instead and win! Keep a steady head in all your life endeavors and drive your opponent crazy. It works every time.

Have you ever been around someone who *lost their head?* Maybe you have used that expression, but it's kind of funny when you say it as you visualize someone really losing their head, running around aimlessly while their head is somewhere else! But when someone loses their cool, going off in a tirade or pity party, it really is sad to watch and be around. Whatever you do, keep a steady head in all you do.

Watch What Your Hands Do, and Where They Go

You would do well to take this to heart. Letting your hands go where they shouldn't be can get you into a whole lot of trouble—in all endeavors of your life!

What you need to do is get a grip on things, whatever you are trying to accomplish. In your life adventure, keeping your hands under control is of the utmost importance. Your hands obey your mind and heart, and many mighty people have fallen because they couldn't control their hands, placing them on something that was forbidden.

Head and hands, both very important parts of your anatomy, and more importantly, how you use them!

But I would have you know,
that the head of every man is Christ.

—1 Corinthians 11:3a

Initiate, Don't Imitate

I can do all things through Christ which strengtheneth me.

—Philippians 4:13

You start your engine!
It's yours to finish.

You Start Your Engine!

Wait a minute, you say, I thought you wanted me to listen to others and learn from them. That's true, you can imitate them some, but remember, you must find your own way, whether in work or play.

Initiate means to begin or originate and that's the way it is. What's so great is that you can do it. I learned that it was like turning the key in the ignition of your car to turn the engine over. Get that engine running, kick it into gear, and take off.

As you apply this to your everyday activity, be the initiator; maybe even the originator. Even if you have a mundane existence, you can make it exciting. Find ways to do it better, do it more efficiently, keep learning and growing. Find what your interest is and pursue that. You can learn from others, but you alone must be your initiator.

It's Yours to Finish

It is sad when someone gives up too easily, and jumps to something else before finishing what they have begun. They can't seem to finish what they started. They might be good starters, but can't get through the hard part, and become poor finishers. I have always thought that I was a pretty good rougher *r*, and could finish what I started, but at times not very well. It isn't easy to finish well all that we start, but we can finish. There is something in the achieving, in making the climb, to reach the summit that is much more exciting than being at the top.

There are times when you will start something you shouldn't have and need to stop before you get well into it; there are other times when you realize early on that you are *in over your head*. Maybe you really hadn't prepared properly for it. Don't hesitate to stop when this happens. Learn from it and don't start something else that you're not sure you can finish.

But remember, it's yours to finish, and initiate, don't imitate.

I can do all things through Christ which strengtheneth me.

—Philippians 4:13

Just Do It

And whatsoever ye do, do it heartily,
as to the Lord, and not unto men.

—Colossians 3:23

If you don't, somebody else will
Some do, and some don't
Don't waste time thinking about it, just do it

If You Don't, Somebody Else Will

There is no doubt about it, that "if you don't, somebody else will" is true! It is close to "he, who hesitates, is lost" or at least, is in jeopardy of losing out. So please do it, whatever it is you have set out to do. You have been educated, you have planned, you have even prayed, now it is time for action. One of the worst things that can happen to anyone is to be a procrastinator, one who keeps putting off doing what they should be doing. I wish it were not so, but I'm afraid there are those who are programming themselves to be lifetime procrastinators.

I'm not an expert in why people do this, but I'm convinced it doesn't have to be. It is something that one has a tendency toward doing, starts practicing it, and then before even they know it, has fallen into the trap. Putting things off can be a killer in getting things done as best as they can be. What amazes me is that the procrastinator can usually get it done at the last minute and somehow get by, but it just can't be the best they can do. You want to be your best, you want to succeed, you want to be head and shoulders above the others, remember: "if you don't, somebody else will."

Some Do, and Some Don't

Some time back, as a young man, I had the privilege of leading a church camp with approximately fifty young people and workers. We had one of the greatest weeks of my life, away from work and golf! At the camp, one of our speakers put on a very funny skit which I don't remember completely, but included these phrases: "If you don't, somebody else will" and "Some do, and some don't." It started out with a fellow on a street corner selling pencils, shouting, "Two for five, two for five." I wish I could remember all of it, but using it in this context, it was very funny.

The moral of "some do, and some don't" is that the achiever will do it, and those who can't or won't, don't do it. You want to be in the category of those who do it, not in those who don't.

Maybe you are convinced that you can't do it, that it is too hard, that someone else could do it better. But in all probability, you do have the wherewithal, you have the ability, you have the opportunity. Don't let the joy pass you by while sitting on the sidelines, get in the game and give it your best shot. You just might surprise yourself and find out you have talents you weren't aware of. Remember "some do, and some don't, and if you don't, somebody else will."

Don't Waste Time Thinking About It, Just Do It

To continue what I have been thinking about and sharing with you, there comes a time for action. Thinking about it any longer won't get it done, and I am thinking here in the context of "just do it." To the best of your ability, make certain the time is right. That might be the hardest part, but it's important to get it as right as you can. To delay might be disastrous. If you don't act now and get the job (or move) done, losing out will be something you might regret for a long, long time.

I still remember clearly some of the more important decisions I made while still pretty young. For instance, when my mom (my dear mother, *mom* was our word of endearment for her) handed out the chore duties, I decided to sign up without hesitation. Maybe it was because she bragged on me, but I did it all as best I could; scrubbing linoleum-covered floors and the wooden baseboards around the floor on my knees, and using the well-worn broom, sweeping walks and porch. You name it, and I did it along with my brothers and sister.

As a teen, I signed on to take a paper route, and it was a big one. Back then we met at a small wooden garage where the papers were dropped off, counting out our papers and placing them in our big bag. I would then put the strap over my shoulder with the bag on my back, and start my route. I was small, and the route was long, but it made me feel good knowing I was doing something a lot of kids my age wouldn't try to do.

I had a couple hundred customers and had to have a drop of more papers on a corner midway through. This meant getting up at 4:00–4:30 every morning, and then after school hurrying to do it all over again (In West Virginia back then, we had some very cold weather with lots of snow). The money had to be collected starting on Thursday evening, continuing on Friday evening, and finishing up on Saturday morning. Wow, I made eleven or twelve dollars a week. I kept a couple dollars and gave the rest to Mom to help buy my clothes and anything else the family needed. It turned out that the paper route was one of the hardest jobs I had in my life, but was one of the best training grounds to prepare me for my future.

One of the most important decisions I made while I was in high school, was to join the civil air cadet patrol program (this is a great program for young people who have an interest in aviation). I fell in love with flying although I had not flown. I just knew I wanted to try it. I took aeronautics and meteorology classes, and I had tried my hand at making model airplanes, and flying them in our yard, some from the front porch roof when we thought mom wouldn't know it.

Belonging to this group helped me in WWII as I signed up for the Aviation Cadet Program in the Army Air Corps. I finally got to fly—a lot and in the B-17 Flying Fortress as a radio operator and waist gunner while in Gunnery School at Yuma, Arizona. Prior to that, while finishing radio school in Sioux Falls, South Dakota, the winter of 1944, two of our training planes collided in midair over our barracks, and crashed, killing ten of our buddies. It was a terrible sight.

I didn't make it overseas, but did a lot of flying while training. When the atomic bomb was dropped in 1945, I was in Lincoln, Nebraska where we were getting ready to go to the Pacific on a B-29.

If you are a young person, you might be facing a decision regarding schooling, or work. You can just do so much research and talking about it; there must come a time for decision. With all the information you can get, and after much prayer and consulting with your parents and others you feel confident in "just do it."

My dad was a good example of this. By today's standards, he wasn't well educated, with an eighth-grade education, but he was smart in his own way. Dad loved to make furniture, and fix up our old house for his family, especially pleasing my mother. He would plan, measure, get his materials together, which many times was scrap lumber from where he worked, and make sure what he was going to do before he did it, driving my mother crazy wondering when he was going to act. Then when it came time for action, he was a whiz a putting it all together. Even in his spare time, he amazed us all with what he did.

> *And whatsoever ye do, do it heartily,*
> *as to the Lord, and not unto men.*
>
> —Colossians 3:23

Keep Your Sense of Humor

Rejoice in the Lord always: and again I say, Rejoice.

—Philippians 4:4

A merry heart does good like a medicine
A broken spirit dries up the bones
A heavy heart is lifted on the wings of Praise

A Merry Heart Does Good Like a Medicine

The source of this is from the Holy Bible, "A merry heart doeth good like a medicine, but a broken spirit drieth the bones" (Proverbs 17:22), and is a wonderful truth. Wouldn't you rather be around people who look on the bright side of life rather than the gloomy? So would others, so find a way to have a merry heart, it will not only do you good like a medicine, it will do good to those you come in contact with also. A merry heart means you have kept your sense of humor! It will do you good like a medicine. It is better than any over the counter or prescription medicine you can find!

How can you keep a merry heart? Will keeping your sense of humor alone be enough? To have, keep and maintain a merry heart, it is important to know the Lord and have full faith in Him. It is easy then to keep your sense of humor, be light hearted and experience the great "medicine" that it provides for your life and soul. You will not only enjoy your life more, but the games you play as well.

We all have games we continue to play; our work might be our "play;" taking care of our homes and families; working out trying to stay fit; and of course playing those games we can keep on playing as we age – soccer, basketball, video game, and golf to name a few.

I have a funny but applicable story to relate to you. We were visiting a relative in Virginia, and her granddaughter Ashley was there, who was about four at the time. As was my nature, I got acquainted with the cute little gal. She wanted me to be here playmate, so I made a paper airplane and we went outside and we were having a good time, until she decided play time was over. She suddenly picked up the paper plane, wadded it into a ball and slammed it to the pavement. I sat down on the curb with my face in my hands pretending to cry. She took a power stance, with her feet spread apart and her hands on her hips, telling me in no uncertain words: "Nobody likes to play with a cry baby!"

With that she was off to her mother, and our relationship had cooled considerably. I have enjoyed relating this story and having a little laugh over it, but there is a great lesson to be learned from my little friend – it is best to have a merry heart and keep your sense of humor – nobody likes to play with a cry baby!

A Broken Spirit Dries up the Bones

Continuing Proverbs 17:22, you will learn what happens when your spirit is broken: it dries up the bones! There is more than one way to have your spirit broken, but one way is to lose your sense of humor. The worst case of broken spirit I suppose is to fail and give up. This allows depression to enter in, and you become a real mess. It's no wonder the bones dry up. They become brittle and break, you can't eat, get up and move about as you should and especially you can't smile. Whatever you do keep a bright, full, vibrant spirit within you – keep your sense of humor, and just possibly you won't end up with "dry" bones!

I had the opportunity to spend the better part of five years trying to help my longtime friend, Ernie, who had fallen into the deep pit of depression. He had let fear become his enemy, and tried to reason his way out of it, but it didn't work. Ernie lost weight, and his shoulders started sagging some; his bones were 'drying up' for a certainty. He was in and out of the hospital several times, almost drove his dear wife nuts, and, although my coaxing and encouraging seemed fruitless, he continued to turn to me, and I welcomed the time we had together. But it was so sad seeing a fun loving friend with a great sense of humor, intelligent, very nice man go into the darkness like that.

Stay in the light of faith and hope, don't try to solve all your very hard problems alone, turn to God and trust Him for the outcome, and hopefully you won't have to experience the terrible disease of depression.

A Heavy Heart is Lifted on the Wings of Praise

This is a wonderful saying I found several years ago. I always try to Praise Him when circumstances or bad news want to cause my heart to become heavy. In fact, with faith believing, it is easy to turn my heart and eyes to heaven and Praise Him who makes it all possible. We don't have anything we haven't received from Him, our Creator, giver of life, and our sustainer. Don't damn him as others do, but Praise Him. He deserves our Praise and it will lift your heavy heart. Try it!

Let me get off my serious vein for a moment and share a little humor with you, this is one of my favorites:

Seems this fellow decided he wanted to "sky dive." He went to the airport to check it out and found an instructor. The instructor told him he could go with a group that very afternoon, he just had to be back early to get the info needed, his parachute and get hooked up. Seems several were going up and he could join them.

He was excited as he got on the plane and when it came his turn to jump, he didn't hesitate long as he was so excited. Out he went, he made his count as instructed, and he gave his rip cord a yank. Nothing happened!! He pulled on the reserve cord and still nothing happened. Suddenly he realized that he was racing toward the earth!

All of a sudden, another guy came up past him going the other way. He cupped his hands around his mouth, and shouted loudly to him, "Do you know anything about parachutes?" He suddenly heard the other guy shouting back, "Do you know anything about gas stoves?" (Gas stoves explode sometimes!)

It might be hard to keep your sense of humor in a situation like that, but you can if you try, and keep you heart and mind on the important things. Learn to laugh at yourself, you will find it won't hurt, and in fact it will help as you are accepted by others. **Remember, make them laugh with you, not at you.**

Rejoice in the Lord always: and again I say, Rejoice.

—Philippians 4:4

Live Life

I press toward the mark for the prize
of the high calling of God in Christ Jesus.

—Philippians 3:14

Don't go through life just existing, but live life
Our lives are like a vapor, we see it and it is suddenly gone
We are here for a purpose, have you found yours?

Don't Go Through Life Just Existing, But Live Life

There are so many people I have known that are wandering aimlessly through life, and I think that is sad. Just existing, living from paycheck to paycheck; no goals, no desire to excel, just seemingly satisfied with "a little less" than the mediocre. These folks can't seem to get excited about anything; they are exercising the status quo. Status quo to me means you are in a rut, described to me as *a grave open at both ends*, and none of us want to be in one of those.

It's more exciting to be involved each day in something you look forward to. That's living life. Work can be like that, it is meant for man to work, but it wasn't meant for man to be dragging through, wondering what being here is all about. Anything you do can be a drag too if you let it, but it doesn't have to be, you need to learn the basics, apply them and develop them to the point where you can enjoy what you are doing, and stay excited about it. One way to do that is to remember that life really is just a game. You don't have to be all uptight about it when it seems like you aren't progressing as well as you think you should be.

Don't go through life just existing, but live life! One way that helps is to remember the other person is important too. Christ taught us that if we want to find our lives, we must lose it; if we would lose our lives, we will find it! He meant that, if we would be happy and truly successful in life, we must have a servant's heart attitude. Try living your life for others and see if this isn't true for you.

Here is another question posed to me, and my answer:

Question: What advice about life do you want others to remember?

Answer: If you look to men you will be disappointed, if you look at self you will be discouraged, if you look at Christ you will be satisfied. Give of yourself. Don't hoard yourself to you, or on yourself. Love the one you say you love (your spouse or parents) by showing them how much you love them, and as best as you can, love them more than you love yourself.

Our Lives Are Like a Vapor, We See It and It Is Suddenly Gone

The Scriptures teach us that life is like a vapor, and also our Lord taught that our lives are like the grass and/or a flower that grows, blooms, and fades away. We need to live life to the fullest, which isn't the same as "eat, drink, and be merry, for tomorrow we die." Living life to the fullest is to be all that you can be, using your full potential in every endeavor. Don't ever tire of hearing this and even reminding yourself of it.

Here is a thought for you: "Time is like our money, they both talk, and they are always saying good-bye."

Here is another question about life put to me by my children:

Share some principles from Scripture on which you have chosen to build your life.

Answer:

Faith—without faith it is impossible to please God.

Marriage—is special to God and honors those who honor their marriage relationship.

The Church—a local body of believers is very special to God and wants us who love Him to be a part of a local assembly.

Children—are a gift from Him.

We are Here For a Purpose, Have You Found Yours?

We really are here for a purpose; if not, we wouldn't have any reason to be here. Our creator God marvelously made these wonderfully complex and intricate bodies and minds of ours. He certainly had a purpose in mind for us. Have you found yours? If you don't do anything else, find out to the best of your ability what it is and pursue it.

There is more to life than just wandering aimlessly around, and then find it is suddenly gone. Find your purpose—live life!

I press toward the mark for the prize
of the high calling of God in Christ Jesus.

—Philippians 3:14

Move or Not to Move

Watch ye, stand fast in the faith, quit you like men, be strong.

—1 Corinthians 16:13

How do I know if I should make a move?

How Do I Know If I Should Make a Move?

Only you can make the decision. But here are just a few questions (there are many more that I won't try to cover here) that you can answer that might be a help. For instance:

Are you comfortable in your present situation?

Comfort isn't the only criteria to look at, but it is a start. You need to think long and hard before making a drastic move; you might be going from the frying pan into the fire!

Are you satisfied with your income?

Once again, money many times isn't the most important thing to consider, but it sure should be high on the list, just don't fall in love with it. (The Bible correctly tells us that 'the love of money is the root of all evil.')

Without it, how do you provide for your family? How do you educate your children? How do you enjoy the life style you have become accustomed to? Look hard at the new income if you make the move, the increased cost of living might be more than you can afford. Is your problem your present work or marriage situation, or could it be your life style?

I'm convinced that we create much of the difficulty we have in life. We make choices that affect us throughout our lifetimes. Many times we make our own beds so to speak, so we have to sleep in them – unless we are willing to make a move, hopefully in the right direction.

Now, let's take a look at one more question: What about leaving your roots, and your family and friends, can you handle that? Maybe you can, and maybe not. I was always thankful that I didn't make a move from my home town like my other sibling brothers did (there were six of us boys) until I was older and retired. But they made a move and it seemed to work out well for them. Many can do that, I didn't think I could. But I often wondered what my life would have been like if I had. In my case, not many opportunities presented themselves. I was able to grow in my job, raise my family in a safe, relatively peaceful environment, and found life exciting. A very important point for you to consider is that you should have a Plan B—something you are interested in that you have taken the time to learn and you can find employment in, if your present job disappears.

But that's me, now how about you? You need to think about all of these as you consider to move or not to move.

So remember move or not to move is important.

Watch ye, stand fast in the faith,
quit you like men, be strong.

—1 Corinthians 16:13

No, I Won't Go There

*Be not deceived; God is not mocked: for whatsoever
a man soweth, that shall he also reap.*

—Galatians 6:7

Going to the wrong place can be disastrous for you
Stop, danger is lurking ahead

Going To the Wrong Place Can Be Disastrous For You

Let me share my idea of what makes a good friend:

Someone who cares, who will listen, and will put up with and overlook your faults. One who will be there when needed, and one you enjoy being with, who has like interest as yourself, and that you can share with. A good friend will be honest with you and won't always agree with you, but you will not dislike them when they don't agree with you.

Most of us get into trouble by listening to and following the wrong people! Especially those who are supposed to be our friends, but if you are being enticed to go to the wrong place, a place you know you shouldn't be, be strong and resist for all you are worth. In life, going to the wrong place can mean going to work at the wrong place for you, or even going to a church that is wrong for you. Have you ever thought of that? My family and I attended a small church for over a year before I realized we were in the wrong place. There was good fellowship and all, but it just wasn't a good fit for us. You want to make sure you are under good, sound Bible teaching, with lots of love and compassion shown for the people from the pastor and his staff.

It has been said that "You can have a bird fly into your hair, but you shouldn't let him build a nest there!" If you find you are in the wrong place, get out as fast as you can, and without too much disruption in your life. Don't let it be disastrous for you.

Stop, Danger Is Lurking Ahead

After being discharged from the Army Air Corps after WWII, I was very unstable. I was still hanging onto my drinking, and my buddies and I liked to hang out at one of the bars in town that had sprung up during the war (just to capitalize on unwary guys like us). I wasn't aware of it at the time, but that was what they were doing. They didn't care much how we behaved, what we said, or who we were with, just so we spent our money! One night, after we had closed the place, and had had enough to drink, one of the fellows suggested we go to a house and join in a party. He insisted that he knew some of the people and all would be fine.

My instinct was to go on home where I belonged, but I gave in to my peers. Turned out that we ended up with a big mess and some fighting. I escaped unharmed, but several didn't. It was a close call for me, and I learned a lesson. I'm so thankful my grandsons haven't had to go through a war or have fallen into the terrible habit of drinking. But have you had some warning signs and didn't heed them? Have you ignored the detour *r* signs in your life? You will have your share of speed bumps in your daily trials and testing, but to not stop when you know you should, can be downright dangerous for you. Each day brings enough trouble all by itself; you need to let that be sufficient and not add to it.

Be sure and look for the detour signs, avoiding the danger that's ahead, and you will feel better about it, believe me. Don't hesitate to stop when danger is lurking.

> *Be not deceived; God is not mocked:*
> *for whatsoever a man soweth, that shall he also reap.*
>
> —Galatians 6:7

Opposition

But now ye also put off all these; anger, wrath, malice.

—Colossians 3:8a

Know who it is you are really opposing

Know Who It Is You Are Really Opposing

Study your opposition, find their strengths and weaknesses, prepare diligently, and plan your attack. After all, in all probability, the person you are really opposing is you! Maybe you never thought of it like that, but it is true. Stop and think about it. In your work life, are you trying to do better than the other fellow to get ahead of him, or are you just trying to better yourself? I'm afraid a lot of folks are opposing someone else, and it hurts them over the long haul.

In my work, in a place of responsibility over a group of people, I knew one of my biggest obstacles was Bob. He was an ex-marine. He was tough and had been a pretty good boxer; one problem was that he hadn't really gotten over it.

We were industrial accountants, and our work was demanding with a lot of pressure, and Bob would erupt, ranting and raving, walking back and forth through the office. He would be allowed to go on like this far too long before our manager would call his hand. But Bob had him bullied, and he kept doing this. He was a capable worker and intelligent, except for his wild tantrums.

After taking over the group, it wasn't too long before Bob took off on one of his tirades. I had prepared for this day, and had my plan ready. I stopped him dead in his tracks before he really got going. This shocked him, and that was exactly what I wanted. Bob was strong and stocky, and could put on a pretty mean face. His fists were clinched. I quietly and politely invited him into my office. I told him I needed to talk to him.

I had a chair ready close to mine and invited him to sit down. By this time, he had calmed down. I looked him in the eye and let him know his days of disrupting the office were over. I let him know that I admired his work and needed him, but couldn't tolerate his behavior; that he was hurting his chances of ever advancing, and that it might get him fired if he ever did it again. I reminded Bob of how much I admired his lovely wife and two beautiful daughters, and I knew he loved them very much. He made life pretty terrible for them, but they stayed with him.

Bob's eyes welled up with tears, and he admitted he had been wrong. I was now shocked, but very relieved. All he needed was an authority figure to stand up to him. His dad had left the family when Bob was young, and he hadn't had a good male role model in his life.

Bob had several relapses, but they were quickly subdued with a look from me, or a quick word to him. We had relative peace and quiet in the office at last.

Study your opposition, find their strengths and weaknesses, prepare diligently, and plan your attack. Know who it is you are really opposing.

But now ye also put off all these; anger, wrath, malice.

—Colossians 3:8a

Prosperity and Protecting

*But my God shall supply all your need according
to his riches in glory by Christ Jesus.*

—Philippians 4:19

You are probably much richer than you think
The most prosperous people I know
Protecting your inheritance

You Are Probably Much Richer Than You Think

A friend of mine used to say, "Boy, I wish I had a million dollars."

I told him, "Wishing won't make it happen, and what would you do if you had a million?"

"I'm not sure," he would say, "but I would like to have it so I could find out."

I told him it would probably just add to his problems, that he might feel like he had to stay up all night to watch it. If he invested it, he would worry about his investment. I don't think he ever gave up though wishing.

Maybe you are like me, I'm working on my second million, I gave up on my first one! Why is it we want to be prosperous, being not quite satisfied with what we have? If you live in these good old United States like I do, you are very wealthy compared to most of the rest of the world, regardless of your station in life. It's just that you might be thinking of prosperity in terms of money only, and don't think you have much. If so, you are dead wrong.

Step back and take stock of what you have. Learn to count your blessings.

First of all, do you have good health, or if not, are you getting adequate care?

Do you have a roof over your head? Are you getting enough to eat? If you are like me, you are probably getting more than you really need.

Do you have friends and/or loved ones near that you can share your life with?

Most importantly, do you have faith in a living, loving God and know that your sins are forgiven? This is the greatest prosperity of all.

You truly are probably much richer than you think.

The Most Prosperous People I Know

We have a good friend who is bound to a wheelchair. She is limited in the use of her arms and hands, but she is bright and smiling. She always has a pleasant word for anyone she meets. She was recently widowed, after over fifty years of marriage, but believe me she is prosperous.

We have known invalids who were bedfast, and poor by today's standards. We would visit them to cheer them up and encourage them, and they always cheered us up! Were they prosperous?

Have you read or heard about the people who overcome great obstacles to succeed? They might not set any records, but they are playing the game, or performing a productive task. These are the most prosperous people I know.

Protecting Your Inheritance

Quickly, suddenly, without much advance notice—that's how many inheritances happen; that's how mine came to me. You might be one who has the advantage of looking forward to yours, as you have someone close in the family who will be leaving their wealth behind, and you hope for, or have been promised, an inheritance. Some get a gift of their inheritance while the person is still living, but that is a gift, and not the kind of inheritance I am talking about.

With my inheritance, there wasn't any advance notice. I didn't know of it being present or available. I wasn't expecting it, and I was living like I didn't even want it. I was totally hopeless when it came to getting my gift of an inheritance.

I don't know if you will receive an inheritance. There are all kinds of inheritances; some are money, some are jewelry, antiques, or property. But whatever your inheritance is, once you get it, you should protect it. Won't you agree?

I will tell you about my inheritance, and how I am protecting it. You really need to hear this, and I want to share it with you.

Here's the kicker, we know there is no free lunch, and there is no free inheritance either; someone has to die before you receive it. Yes, some get a gift of an inheritance prior to one dying, like the prodigal son in the Bible, but it isn't the norm, and most of the time it is wasted by the one getting it.

In the way of background, and as I have said earlier, I was raised in a good family, with loving parents, and a bunch of siblings. I knew about Jesus. I heard about him in Sunday school and church. We didn't talk about him much at home, except to be taught that we shouldn't take God's name in vain, or swear in God's name. I grew up with the fear that I would slip up and say a swear word about God. That is, after I learned to, and liked to cuss. I got pretty good at cussing, and thought it made me look bigger than I was. I was wrong of course, and I hope you don't fall into that trap. I didn't know what would happen to me if I did blurt out a swear word, and I didn't want to find out.

The important thing I want you to know is that I *knew* about Jesus, but I didn't really *know* Him. There is a big difference. I had heard about his dying at a young age, and how he had lived a good life. It didn't really mean much to me, as he wasn't my grandpa, or rich uncle, you see, so I just went cruising along in my own carefree way.

In my mind, I believed that he died, and I kind of believed that he came back to life. I fussed about getting dressed up, but thought it was neat to go to church with my family on Easter Sunday morning like everyone else. But there was no feeling in my heart that it had anything to do with me. I thought about it some, but not too much. I was having too much fun.

Receiving an inheritance is very exciting, especially when it is not expected. Inheritances are ours to keep and use however we want to. One thing we need to do is to protect any inheritance we get, and use it wisely.

It was a special day for me when I learned that I had received an inheritance. It dawned on me that my inheritance was mine alone, it had no strings attached to it, and all the provisions had been taken care of. All I had to do was accept it, protect it, and fully enjoy it.

My inheritance was everlasting, it couldn't ever be used up, rust out, get old, or disappear. You can imagine how excited I was to know that I had received it. Having now received my inheritance, I knew *who* Jesus was, not just know *about* him. I knew what He had done for me, to provide me my inheritance!

Have you ever imagined what it would be like to have a rich relative that you didn't know you had, and that he/she had remembered you in their will? Your ship had come in, and you were getting onboard!

I found out that Jesus was a close relative of mine, and had left me an inheritance when he died. Once again let me tell you, I had known about Jesus, but now I knew him personally and up close. In fact, he was my father. No, not my earthly father, but my heavenly Father! I found out that he knew all about me and loved me enough to die for me. That is real love. Suddenly, I went from being a loser, to being in a win-win situation!

How It Became Mine!

Let me tell up front, it didn't become mine when Jesus died, as he died for everyone, not just me. He died for you too. My inheritance became mine when I accepted it as mine. It's like someone leaving a sizeable check made out to you at your bank, and letting you know about it, but you don't really own it until you endorse it (claim it as yours), and deposit it in your account. You can then start enjoying it. It would be sad if you knew about it being there for you, and you didn't do your part and accept it. Don't you agree?

That's how it was for me. Jesus had died and left me an inheritance, but I had not claimed it as my very own. When I found out it was mine, and all I had to do was believe he had provided it for me when he died, I was overwhelmed with joy. I claimed it and received it. It is mine, and no one can take it away from me!

How Am I Protecting My Inheritance?

That is a good question, and I will answer it, as you need to know. Knowing that I got my inheritance from his death for me, and that was such a great price he paid, I want to do everything I can to protect it.

First, I guard it from any danger that is lurking about trying to steal it from me. I know the enemy, the old Devil, is out there, so I try to always know where I am going, and who I am with, what I say, and how I behave. If I don't, I might open the door for the enemy to enter in.

Knowing for a fact that Jesus rose up from the dead, and is in heaven watching over me, I try to stay in close contact with him. I pray, ask his help in my life and for his forgiveness. He always comes through for me.

Besides all that, when I found out that God is love, and full of grace, I knew that he had given me faith to believe. I am now confident, and assured of my inheritance so it is easy for me to protect it. I don't let my guard down, I stay all prayed up, and in close contact with him by reading his word he gave me—the Bible.

Let me ask you a question, "If you would wake up tomorrow morning, and found all your neighbors, friends, and family who were Christians, had suddenly disappeared, would you be shocked?" I know you would. It is going to happen someday, and if it happens to you, you are on the other side of the rapture of the church. You will know the rapture has happened when you see all the violence, the turmoil, and the tribulation that is surrounding you.

The rapture happens when Jesus comes back and takes all who have believed in him, who have claimed him as their own, and takes them home with him to heaven. He raptures them out of this world.

That would be a real shock and a shame, to find yourself on the other side of the rapture. But the good news is that you don't have to miss out, it is not too late to still get the inheritance Jesus has provided for you. Remember, I told you that Jesus died for everyone, not just a few, but it is sad that just a few accept his offer, and what he did for them to have everlasting life. You can claim him right now and have your inheritance.

Go to Jesus, call out to him, confess to him that you know you are lost, and can't save yourself, and ask him to forgive you. You will receive your inheritance. Once you get your inheritance, you can start enjoying it and protecting it.

You will be glad you did, and Jesus will too!

But my God shall supply all your need according to his riches in glory by Christ Jesus.

—Philippians 4:19

Questioning

Do all things without murmurings and disputings.

—Philippians 2:14

There aren't any stupid questions
Questioning with good timing
Questioning along with listening

There Aren't Any Stupid Questions

I've heard this said all of my life, but I'm not so sure. Some sound pretty stupid, don't they? Those that seem redundant, rhetorical, or have obvious answers, sometimes sound stupid. Maybe the word stupid is too harsh, most questions are asked in the hope of getting an intelligent answer.

I'll ask you one, how smart is it to not ask questions, when you are learning and need information? I would say not too smart, and I hope you agree. Don't be afraid to ask questions, whether it sounds stupid or not, it will be more stupid if you don't ask them. Maybe there aren't any stupid questions after all.

Questioning With Good Timing

It won't do you much good if you ask a question when you aren't thinking about or trying to do what you are trying to learn, your timing is off. If you are a good note taker, and your teacher is a patient person, it might work, but not as well as asking the question while you are actually doing the action, with good timing.

Timing is important in most everything we do, and getting our questions out in the open and answered is one of them. In your work, you don't want to be left hanging to do a job you still have important questions about. You will be frustrated and not be able to produce a finished product without those answers.

Questioning Along With Listening

This brings us to questioning along with listening. Listen closely to the answers, and put them into practice. Listening is probably more important than talking, while carrying on a conversation. While you are talking, chances are you aren't really learning much. Learn to be a good listener. It isn't easy, I have tried to learn this through the years, and it is something you have to work on all the time. It will pay off for you if you really make a concerted effort to be a questioner, along with listening.

Do everything without murmuring or disputings.

—Philippians 2:14

Repetition, Repetition

Finally, brethren whatsoever things are true, honest, just, pure, lovely, of good report, if there be any virtue, or any praise, think on these things.

—Philippians 4:8 abbreviated

Repetition isn't a bad thing!
Don't close your mind!
Get your body in tune with your brain!

Repetition Isn't a Bad Thing!

Repetition, repetition can't be overemphasized. It is akin to location, location, location when you want to buy or sell your home, if you are an adult and have that need. Maybe you have been there and done that. But it just can't be overemphasized. In your learning, don't be hesitant or draw back from repetition.

It has been said that to form a habit you must do it at least three times or it won't stay with you. For some, like me, three usually wasn't enough. I had to write things down and go back through my notes as I learned how to do the task. I had completed all of the class work I needed, but my work as a cost accountant in a large industrial plant meant learning all about the production of our products and calculating the costs to manufacture over ten thousand different items. It was challenging and exciting, and without applying repetition to my learning I couldn't have been successful.

So, whatever you do, don't hesitate to repeat, repeat, and repeat again your action. You will soon see some results and start feeling good about yourself, as your confidence improves.

Remember, repetition isn't a bad thing!

Don't Close Your Mind

The natural instinct is to say to yourself, "I've heard all of this before. I don't need to hear it again." Chances are you do, and it will do you good to listen carefully. Something will be said that you hadn't picked up before and you aren't using. Don't close your mind.

A closed mind is like a closed book, you won't get much use out of it if it isn't open! Hardheadedness has caused many to fail. They had the basic know-how, and for some strange reason though that was enough. There is always room for learning regardless of how smart you think you are. And there is always someone who is a little smarter than you are. You can bet on that, and you can learn from them if you won't get too hardheaded. The problem seems to be that pride (or stupidity maybe) will tell you not to listen to them, that you already know enough. Please, whatever you do, don't close your mind.

"All of this repetition is boring," you might say, "Why do I have to listen to this again?" There could be several reasons. One being that you haven't taken the time, or had the time, to practice it enough to get it ingrained into your being. One other reason is that (if you are like me and millions of others) you forget. You think you have learned something, but when it comes time to use it, you can't do it as well as you think you could.

So, keep an open mind, and you will be amazed what else you will learn from something you thought you already knew.

Get Your Body In Tune With Your Brain!

Repetition will help you to do this. Repetition is one of the basic tools of learning, and the more we repeat an action, the closer our bodies get in tune with our brains. As you are learning something new, maybe you heard it once and performed it once, and thought you had it. When you go back later to do it, it isn't there. What happened? If you had taken the time to write it down and repeat it several times, chances are you would have had it the next time. Don't be afraid to make notes. I know, it takes a little longer, but the writing of it goes a long way in helping you to remember it. And the repeating of it gets the body in tune with the brain.

> *Finally, brethren whatsoever things are true, honest,*
> *just, pure, lovely, of good report, if there be any virtue,*
> *or any praise, think on these things.*

—Philippians 4:8 abbreviated

Seek

But seek ye first the kingdom of God,
and his righteousness; and all these things shall
be added unto you.

—*Matthew 6:33*

Seek your own level of ability
Seek beyond your level; reach for a higher one

Seek Your Own Level of Ability

Your ability, or abilities, won't be the same as others. If you're not careful, you will be jealous if you know someone who seems to have more going for them than you do. Jealousy is a killer; don't let jealousy enter into your thinking, and become a part of you. It is sneaky and can be in before you realize it. That's why I say to seek your own level of ability. Chances are that if you apply all the other advices given in this book, you will succeed, even with less ability.

Let's think about your abilities. You might be asking, how do I know what my abilities are? To help you answer that, you need to answer the following questions:

What do I really enjoy doing? This is other than sleeping and goofing off, most of us really enjoy those things. Think of activities that are of a constructive and/or productive nature.

What am I good at? In school, did you excel in math or English, or did you like history? What about sports, were you pretty good and really liked some?

Do I like to compete? Not all do, you know. It is good to know how important this is to you, to strive to win or best an opponent. Maybe that isn't your cup of tea at all, and you are satisfied to just be in the game.

These are questions you need to answer for yourself. If you are doing something or striving for something now that doesn't meet the criteria above, you need to consider changing your choices. If you don't change, you might get stuck in a career choice not of your liking.

Find out what you're abilities are and seek your own level in those!

Seek Beyond Your Level, Reach For a Higher One

Let's assume you have reached a plateau, a level of success. It's time to reach higher, don't be satisfied with mediocrity. That first level is mediocre compared to what you can really do. As you continue to seek beyond your present level, you will revel in your measure of success. This will instill confidence to go on to a higher plane and a more secure future.

This, along with an expression of thankfulness to the Lord, and all those around you who have helped make it possible, will help make your life more complete and fulfilling. You will enjoy life more, and your family, friends, and coworkers will enjoy you more too.

But seek ye first the kingdom of God,
and his righteousness; and all these things shall
be added unto you.

—Matthew 6:33

Think

*Which of you by taking thought
can add one cubit unto his stature?*

—Matthew 6:27

Just thinking about something won't be enough
While you are thinking, think rightly

Just Thinking About Something Won't Be Enough

Actions speak louder than words! My dear mother instilled that into me, and it's something I have heard all my life. I have said it many times too, especially to my children while they were growing up. But it is so true! You can think about something until you are exhausted, but it just won't help you to get it done. This is so obvious, but so many people seem to never get the message. They are the so-called "heavy thinkers," the intellectual type maybe, but they aren't the heavy producers.

I think I can, I think I can! Okay get going and prove to yourself and others that you really can. My dad used to have a little low whistle while he was thinking, and if he had his felt hat on, always pushed it back on his head. He would think things out completely before starting. Once he got started, there was no stopping him until he finished the job, and he always did an excellent job.

While You Are Thinking, Think Rightly

It is best to stop and think before speaking.

I like this acronym for THINK, and try to practice it:

T—Is it true?
H—Is it honest?
I—Is it inspiring?
N—Is it necessary?
K—Is it kind?

Stay on target with your thinking. This isn't as easy as it sounds; there are all kinds of distractions that creep in to get you thinking wrongly. You have to learn to concentrate, to zero in on what you want to do, and while you are thinking, think rightly.

Don't let your thinking get disrupted, letting your mind wander off on tangents that won't contribute to what you are trying to do. This trap is so easy to fall into, and if it happens, the first thing you know you are way behind. Stop as quickly as you recognize the trap and get back on track.

Just thinking about something won't be enough, and while you are thinking, think rightly.

> *Which of you by taking thought can add*
> *one cubit unto his stature?*

—Matthew 6:27

Utilize

He that covereth his sins shall not proper;
but whoso confesseth and forsaketh them shall have mercy.

—Proverbs 28:13

Utilize your full potential
Utilize all the tools available to you
Utilize the natural abilities you have been given

Utilize Your Full Potential

A kind old gentleman friend of mine who had a corner gas station and car repair shop near where I lived, hired young boys part time to help out. He had a couple of them working one day. I was there waiting for my car. The boys were horse playing a little bit, and I could see some frustration building up in my friend. He came over to where I was, pushed his grease-stained felt hat back, and said, "I found out that if you have a boy, you have a boy, but if you have two boys, you have half a boy, and if you have three boys, you don't have a boy at all!" I had a good laugh with him, and agreed totally. After all, I had been a boy once with five brothers, so I knew exactly what he was talking about.

It seems that guys especially have a way of never completely growing up. You might find yourself horse playing around, letting your work go to pot. You won't be utilizing your full potential.

I have known young people though who were mature beyond their years and started accomplishing much at an early age. It doesn't have to be all fun and games, although they surely have a place. It's okay to have fun, and have a good time, but don't let it rob you of utilizing your full potential.

Utilize All the Tools Available To You

As a boy, I couldn't believe all the tools my dad had, and he used most of them. Dad loved to tinker and build things, and back in those days, they were "hand" tools, not the powered kind we have today. I found out that having the right tool increases the percentage of success in completing a task.

Most of the tools today are high powered, and many of a technologic nature. Most of these are lightweight, made of plastic, etc. but they are mighty powerful in the hands of those who know how to use them. I've come to the conclusion that to finish a task, that at least 75 percent of the going into it has to be the equipment or tools; the other 25 percent being knowledge or ability. But you think about it, you might think the numbers should be reversed.

Get the tools and utilize them. They won't do you much good if you don't use them.

Utilize the Natural Abilities You Have Been Given

Have you ever thought how wonderful it is that you can do what you do, regardless if you are the best or not? You have been given those abilities, so utilize them to their fullest. You have the potential, the tools, and your natural abilities so put them to good use.

One great way to utilize your natural abilities is to do all you can to develop them. Find out what your interests are, what you are good at, and pursue that. You can do it.

He that covereth his sins shall not prosper; but whoso confesseth and forsaketh them shall have mercy.

—Proverbs 28:13

View the Big Picture

Set your affection on things above, not on things on the earth.

—Colossians 3:2

One battle does not make a war
Don't limit your scope of the task at hand

One Battle Does Not Make a War

The truthful saying, "You can win the battle, but lose the war," can be applied to work you are doing. You can argue to make your point (that you feel confident is correct) and convince others to accept your position while beating them down. If you are not listening to them, or accepting their point of view, you just might lose that person's respect for the future when you will need them the most.

One battle does not make a war. You have to stay on course, winning one battle after another. Life is a struggle, but if you stop with winning a few battles and not them all, you will have lost the war. Try to keep the big picture focused in your mind, as you are learning to listen to the other person's point of view, and be able to make the right decision.

Don't Limit Your Scope of the Task At Hand

It's amazing the difference a wide-angle lens makes in photography. You know what it means to "see the big picture." And you no doubt have heard the expression: "He is too close to the forest to see the trees!" That can happen if your focus is with tunnel vision on something, and you limit your scope of the task at hand.

There will be times when you might be so involved in one area of what you are doing that you have neglected some other very important part. Without that part you won't be able to complete the job. You have limited your scope of the task at hand. Stop where you are and get everything done so you can finish with a completed product to present to your teacher or boss.

Whatever you do, don't limit your scope of the task at hand.

Set your affection on things above,
not on things on the earth.

—Colossians 3:2

Want More

And if a man also strive for masteries,
yet he is not crowned, except he strive lawfully.

—2 Timothy 2:5

Don't be satisfied with a mundane existence

Don't Be Satisfied with a Mundane Existence

Don't get me wrong, I'm not talking about greed when I tell you to want more than you are getting. Greed brings people down all the time, from all walks of life! It has been the downfall of lots of people who seem to have it all: wealth, fame, everything the world has to give. What a shame when you see them in the news caught up in some illegal activity trying to make more money, or get more excitement or satisfaction, that they think they need. Their hard-earned reputations are tarnished! Their lives are anything but mundane, but you wouldn't want to trade places with them.

We have had two of our former governors in our home state sent to prison because of greed coupled with power-seeking and just plain old corruption. The human psyche is capable of causing us to do some really stupid, bad things. Don't be satisfied with the mundane, but don't allow greed to overtake you either.

In your life work, complacency can be a real detriment to your becoming better. The mundane breed's boredom, boredom complacency, and complacency will cause your progress to slow way down.

And if a man also strive for masteries,
yet he is not crowned, except he strive lawfully.

—2 Timothy 2:5

X—Let It Mean Excel

Let us draw near with a true heart in full assurance of faith.

—Hebrews 10:22a

Strive for excellence
Put all of these ABC's into practice
Don't be satisfied with less than the best for your life

Strive For Excellence

This is the opposite of settling for the status quo, which complacency loves. Commit all that you have to performing the best you can. Achieve all that you want to within reason, while not hurting those around you. Be careful not to hurt others, maybe even those who you are striving so hard to provide for. Whatever you do, don't do that.

Striving for excellence means you won't be satisfied with less than your best in all that you do.

Put All of These ABC's Into Practice

I honestly believe you will be happier and accomplish more in life if you practice these simple ABC's (I have purposely tried to not be too heavy or difficult to understand, I wouldn't have enjoyed doing that anyway), otherwise I wouldn't bother to share them with you. One thing you have to remember when things seem to be falling apart is to get back to the basics. Get back to what worked best for you to get you where you are. You have no doubt noticed that how all of these tips are very basic. Sometimes we are better off without so much verbiage and technical jargon. I hope you are already putting these ABC's into practice.

Don't Be Satisfied With Less Than the Best For Your Life

I'm not suggesting that you should be dissatisfied, unless you are doing less than the best you can. Don't get down on yourself unless you are doing something that isn't the best for your life. That can happen, and maybe it is happening to you. If so, don't be satisfied with less than the best for your life.

Let us draw near with a true heart
in full assurance of faith.

—Hebrews 10:22a

You Are Who You Are

*Examine yourselves, whether ye be
in the faith; prove your own selves.*

—2 Corinthians 13:5a

You know by now that you can't be anyone else
Look inside your heart, and find the real you

You Know by Now That You Can't Be Anyone Else

I have said this before, but you are truly who you are, it is a simple statement and so obvious, but so many don't live like they know it. It is fine to emulate and learn from others, to learn from others' mistakes they say, but usually you have to make your own mistakes and hopefully learn thereby.

Why would you want to be anyone else? God made you just like you are, with all your bumps and warts, with your great or little talent. So if you try to be someone who seems to have it all together, you will be disappointed and frustrated. Besides, the world will see through your vain attempts, and you will eventually feel further rejection. It just doesn't work.

Look Inside Your Heart, and Find the Real You

You have heard this phrase before, I'm sure: "Look inside yourself," but what does that mean, anyway? I am going to take a shot at it, by saying it means first of all to look at your heart, the seat of your emotions. Is your heart in tune with what you are doing with your life? Solomon shared wisdom with us in Proverbs 3:5, 6. This is my paraphrase for you: If you trust in the Lord with all your heart, and you are not depending solely on your own understanding, if you acknowledge him in all your ways, He will direct your path. Do you really have a "heartfelt" desire to excel, to grow, to continue in what you are doing? Trusting the Lord for guidance will help you in every way.

Look inside to your thinking; are you satisfied with what you find? Have you become lax in your speech, letting slang and/or profanity spew forth, in your attempt to be someone you aren't? You won't impress anyone, and others will look on you with disdain and disappointment. Remember, you are who you are.

Examine yourselves, whether ye be
in the faith; prove your own selves.

—2 Corinthians 13:5a

Zeal

The LORD is my rock, and my fortress, and my deliverer;
my God, my strength, in whom I will trust; my buckler,
and the horn of my salvation, and my high tower.

—Psalm 18:2

Zeal is enthusiasm. Enthusiasm is important in all that you do Finally, last but not least, is zeal. If you are zealous in your achieving, you will be enthusiastic also. Enthusiasm is contagious, and can produce a synergistic effect where one plus one equals three, bringing about greater results.

Bob, the ex-marine boxer I told you about who worked for me, and a group of us were playing golf in a company-sponsored league at Riviera golf course in an after-work league. It was just nine holes, but it might as well have been twenty-seven for Bob. He was zealous all right, but it was misplaced enthusiasm, mostly because he tried too hard to do something he didn't have the talent or ability to do. Poor Bob (and the poor guys who had to play with him) attacked the ball like he did the punching bag at the gym, and his frustration level rose with each hole. After several weeks of this struggle, one day Bob walked off number twelve green after a triple or quadruple bogey, red-faced but containing his anger. He calmly unhooked the straps that were holding his bag on his walk-around golf cart. He let the bag fall to the ground, picked up the cart with both hands, held it high over his head, and went screaming to the edge of a bank leading down to a creek. He heaved the cart as far as he could, and watched briefly as the cart went tumbling into the ravine below. He turned, huffing and puffing, while brushing his hands together, as if he had taken care of his problem. Bob carried his clubs the rest of the round but sadly nothing had improved.

It's the same way in your life work, be zealous and your enthusiasm will help you produce more; be happier in what you do, and you will set a good example for others. But whatever you do, don't have misplaced zeal like poor old Bob.

The LORD *is my rock, and my fortress, and my deliverer;*
my God, my strength, in whom I will trust; my buckler,
and the horn of my salvation, and my high tower.

—Psalm 18:2

Conclusion

This has been an enjoyable experience for me, and we both know that I could have written much more; the much more is what you will write with your life.

This will be beneficial to you in whatever endeavor you undertake if applied.

There are no real-life experts, but there are many like me who have lived a lot of it, and it is one thing we never stop learning how to do.

The Lord has given me a little wisdom, so I am glad to share it with you. Someday you might be called upon to share some of yours with others. Live your life with gusto and high standards, and you will be prepared to answer the call.

One of the greatest blessings I received while serving the Lord as a lay person in church was leading teens and young adults. My wife and I had that privilege for well over twenty years. Some of those youngsters are grandparents today, and we stay in touch with several of them. Why was it a blessing? We gave of our lives to them, we mentored them. Doing so gave our children many happy hours meeting with us. They gave of themselves and learned a lot in the process.

We are still mentoring while older. Just this last year, a young married couple moved in next to us, and we got acquainted. They were from Uzbekistan, had university degrees, and had completed their PhDs here in this country. Truly, an amazing accomplishment, and we are proud of them.

They wanted to learn about our faith, so we shared with them with Bible study and attending church together. We had a wonderful year with them, and they are good friends of ours although now living in another state. They are most appreciative of our mentoring, and we are blessed with their friendship and love for us.

During this same time, we met a lovely lady who worked near us, of Vietnamese descent, and her boyfriend who joined us in our study. These four were a great blessing to us, as they responded to the teaching and mentoring.

So my suggestion to you is to mentor as you are mentored. Listen and learn from those trying to help you, and be patient with those you try to help.

Remember, it all starts with "Attitude," and ends with "Zeal," with a whole lot of other important things in between. Practice them all, you can even makeup some of your own, maybe better than mine that are more applicable to you.

Whatever you do, do it the best you know how. As much as possible, enjoy everything you do. Stay honest in your dealings. Be truthful in your words, don't let the material things of the world dominate your life.

An old cliché says, "The best things in life are free." That's true, as they are freely given to us by our precious Lord and creator; all for our benefit to have and enjoy. So, keep your eye on the prize. You can have an eternal place of rest and peace the same as I do, just reach out and accept it from His gracious hand.

Our lives consist of actions and reactions, of good or adverse circumstances and our responses to them. Some of you, regardless of your age, might have already faced adversity or grief through the loss of a loved one or friend. I surely hope this is not true in your life, but it will. How will you react when it happens?

As a teen, my time for reaction happened when my dear mother fell down the steps and broke her leg. I visited her in the hospital, and after a few seconds at the foot of her bed, seeing the stress in her face, and her suspended cast and rods extending from each side of her foot, I made a speedy exit before I fainted!

Still a teen and in the Army Air Corps, my dear grandfather whom I loved died, and I was not allowed to leave my base for his funeral. This was very painful for me, and I hated my commanding officer for not understanding, but I was learning that rules "are not made to be broken," as some have suggested, and I had to accept his decision.

The longer you live, as I have, you will have many upheavals in your life. My reactions were hard to get through before I was a Christian. After I accepted Jesus into my heart, I found I could take my heartache, grief, pain, and suffering to Him, and that made it so much easier to go through the darkness. He is light and life, and He will give you light for your journey, if you will just let Him.

May God bless you and keep you
L. A. Burner
my Blog: www.uncleburnie.wordpress.com
E-address: lb.gbcouple@gmail.com